P9-DNS-576

Animals Work

by TED LEWIN

I Like to Read®

Holiday House / New York

To the children and animals of Green Chimney
Farm and Wildlife Center

I LIKE TO READ is a registered trademark of Holiday House, Inc.

Copyright © 2014 by Ted Lewin
Map copyright © 2014 by Holiday House, Inc.
All Rights Reserved
HOLIDAY HOUSE is registered in the U.S. Patent and Trademark Office.
Printed and Bound in March 2014 at Tien Wah Press, Johor Bahru, Johor, Malaysia.
The artwork was created with pencil, watercolor, and liquid mask on Strathmore Bristol.
www.holidayhouse.com
First Edition
1 3 5 7 9 10 8 6 4 2

Library of Congress Cataloging-in-Publication Data
Lewin, Ted.
Animals work / by Ted Lewin.
pages cm. — (I like to read)
ISBN 978-0-8234-3040-6 (hardcover)
1. Working animals—Juvenile literature. I. Title.
SF172.L49 2014
591.5—dc23
2013014333

A dog herds.

A horse carries.

Camels carry.

A donkey carries.

A donkey pulls.

A reindeer pulls.

Oxen pull.

A goat pulls.

An elephant lifts.

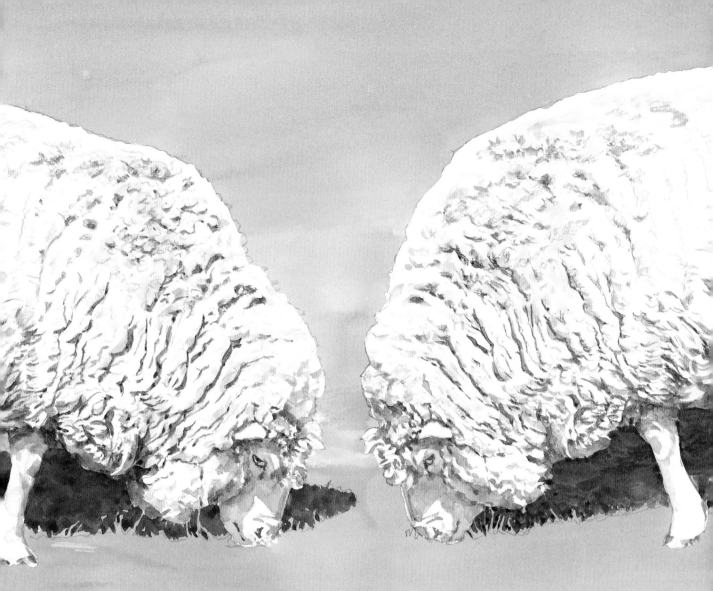

Sheep mow.

Llamas keep sheep safe.

My cat keeps me company.

And I care for my cat.

Also by Ted Lewin

Can You See Me?

Look!

★"A satisfying challenge and a fun animal adventure made thrilling by Lewin's characteristically spectacular use of light."
—*Kirkus Reviews* (starred review)

What Am I? Where Am I?

"Animals bristle with photo-realistic fur, and they are captured in wonderfully textured environments and positions that make them seem to breathe on the page."
—*Booklist*

Visit www.holidayhouse.com/I-Like-to-Read/ for more about I Like to Read®
books, including flash cards, reproducibles, and the complete list of titles.

Where Ted Saw the Animals

DISCARD